MW01296029

The
Angels
on Our
Doorstep

Jo Anne Tressler

Copyright © 2021 Jo Anne Tressler
All rights reserved
First Edition

PAGE PUBLISHING, INC.
Conneaut Lake, PA

First originally published by Page Publishing 2021

ISBN 978-1-6624-4953-6 (pbk)
ISBN 978-1-6624-4954-3 (digital)

Printed in the United States of America

To my mom and dad and my husband for all of their love, support, and hard work. They helped turn what could have been a disaster into a happy ending.

Be not forgetful to entertain strangers, for thereby
some have entertained angels unawares.
—Hebrews 13:2

Chapter 1

The roads we travel are circuitous and sometimes appear to be dead ends, even when we think we have a map and a plan. Fortunately, for some of us, life tends to step in and lead us to our true destination and ultimately our reason for being.

Those fortunate people who knew from a very young age who they were, what they wanted, and their purpose in life seemed to me as if they were sprinkled with unicorn dust. At the age of thirty-six, I was still wondering if my life truly held meaning.

My husband, Marc, and I had been married for sixteen years, owned a home, and both had good jobs that we enjoyed. Everything was as it should be, but I still felt there was some elusive element just out of reach.

Marc's job with Linde Air was challenging and fulfilling. He had recently begun to travel around the country, closing plants for complete maintenance (called a turnaround) and then restarting them. His first love, however, was farming. Every winter, he spent weeks pouring over countless seed catalogs, searching for just the right combination of garden plants.

Our first spring brought with it our first garden. We didn't have much in the line of farming equipment, so Marc called for support in the form of Earl Johnson with his ponies and plow.

Earl lived nearby and liked opportunities to work his little team. We could depend on him to come armed with lots of great stories.

We relied on him our first couple of springs and looked forward to his arrival each time with great anticipation. The plowing never took very long, but the stories could entertain us for quite a while. Once Earl and the ponies were headed back down the road, the next challenge was to level the freshly plowed earth. Marc didn't have a disc, but he did have an old set of bed springs. However, they weren't heavy enough by themselves to do the trick.

The first year, he managed to talk me into stretching out on the springs to hold them down while he pulled them with his little garden tractor. It didn't take too much bouncing and pounding over the furrows to convince me that wasn't the solution. We then loaded the springs up with every rock and anything else we could find with any weight, which proved much more successful.

He began slowly the first year, growing only tomatoes and potatoes. Within a few short years, he progressed into supplying a friend's elaborate annual Halloween displays with pumpkins, squash, Indian corn, gourds, broom corn, and popcorn. Our three acres were shrinking rapidly.

We had been talking for several years about buying a farm someday. He wanted more land, and I wanted more space. We had spent our entire marriage next door to a neighbor who was closer in age to our parents, and I believe he was goodhearted, but he did his best to make our business his own. His relentless questions about us, our families, friends, and constant interference in everything we did had grown exasperating. At one time, he explained to Marc that he was raised with the belief that unless a person's family had been known by his family for at least two generations, they were to be considered strangers and consequently untrustworthy. The first six years, I played along, thinking sooner or later he would learn everything he felt he needed to know. The last ten had worn me down. I longed for the status of a complete stranger.

Then there were the neighbors who I found filling water jugs from our outdoor spigot one day when I came home unexpectedly.

That in itself wasn't terrible, although it did seem odd since we had never even met before that day. But it did raise the inevitable question: "What else were they doing while we were at work?"

Their peacock added another dimension to the relationship when he chose to roost on our garage roof and, in the mornings, shriek at us when we exited the house.

One day, our friend, Mike Smith, took us for a ride down a little side road we hadn't even realized was there. We stopped at an old rundown farm that was coming up for sale. His boyhood friend had grown up there, and the mother was preparing to move to Florida.

We received only a quick tour of the property, but for us, it was love at first sight.

The first thing I noticed was the open space. I could see only one house, and it was nearly an eighth of a mile away. In every direction, there were either woods or open fields of corn, wheat, or hay. The one-lane dirt road that traveled past the farm disappeared into a woods a fourth of a mile away. It all seemed too good to be true.

For sixteen years, we had been living four miles from our idea of a little slice of heaven. It was remote; it had a pond, two pine groves, a creek, a circular drive, and no neighbors. It had three buildings that consisted of a house, a garage that looked as if it could blow over with a little wind, and a milk house. Of the three buildings, the milk house looked the most stable. Undaunted, we couldn't wait to show off our new purchase to our parents. We expected them to be as elated as we were. Our excitement was met with shocked looks and stunned silence.

It wasn't until years later that my mother confided in me the distress she felt on her first visit.

She said she finally understood the despair my grandmother from Chicago felt when she burst into tears upon viewing my parents' "new" home decades earlier. The coal stove in the middle of the living room and the outhouse in the backyard had proved too much for her. I'm grateful my mother exhibited more self-control at our farm. Her main concern was that Marc traveled extensively with his job, and I would be out there all alone, which didn't strike me as a drawback.

We had indoor plumbing, but the roof, siding, walls, ceilings, floors, wiring, furnace, pump, kitchen cabinets, bathroom, light fixtures, plumbing, doors, and windows all needed to be replaced.

Upon closer inspection, Marc also noticed the north wall of the kitchen had come loose from the foundation and was beginning to buckle. That alone was quite intimidating, but in spite of it all, the location still buoyed our spirits.

One of the men who helped to work the farmland around us said he always thought of it as an oasis. The house, with its circular drive lined with pines, was surrounded by four one-hundred-year-old maple trees. Those stalwart sentinels hugged and shaded the house, still guarding it from the elements just as they had done for so many decades.

We were advised by more than one friend and several contractors that a bulldozer was the best solution to all our problems with the house. There were many days during the next year that those words came back to haunt us.

I clearly remember the Sunday afternoon that my parents made an unannounced visit. They discovered the bathtub sitting in the backyard and us, saturated with plaster dust, shoveling plaster from the kitchen walls out the back door and into our dump truck. They came prepared for anything and pitched right in.

Once the plaster on the north wall of the kitchen was exposed, we found etched in the wall the year 1883 and the initials *JP*. Since the kitchen appeared to be an addition to the main part of the house, it gave us some idea of the overall age of the structure. We salvaged that part of the wall, and my dad and Marc made an oak frame that now hangs nearly in the same spot where it was etched so long ago. To this day, we still don't know the identity of JP.

Marc felt confident about handling the destruction part of the scenario, with a crowbar and sledgehammer being the main tools required. However, the rebuilding and replacement that loomed before us was daunting. Fortunately, my dad also saw the potential charm of the place and wanted to become actively involved. He was a jack-of-all-trades, and over the years, he had remodeled their house into a beautiful home. He was retired and more than willing to help us in every way possible. As a result, he spent nearly every weekend here for the next year, orchestrating the entire project. He and Marc became very close during that time, and "Gramps," as he was known only to Marc, shared much of his carpentry knowledge with his son-in-law.

Never one to be outdone, my mom was also available most weekends and willing to help. Pulling into the drive dressed in her work clothes and gloves, she would come equipped with everything she thought we might need that day, whether it was cleaning supplies, sandpaper, brushes and rollers, or wallpapering tools. She was also known to occasionally appear with a hot meal or at least sandwiches for the famished workers. My parents were dedicated to the monumental task before us. I can't imagine what we would have done without them.

Choosing not to live in the house during the remodeling phase, we opted to remain in our old house, thus avoiding plaster dust and sawdust seeping into every crevice of our possessions.

We understood the value of having a place to escape to and relax. The relief in being able to close one door on near chaos and open another with a place to sit down and a clean bed to sleep in proved immeasurable. Marc worked tirelessly every evening and every weekend. It evolved into his personal quest.

Looking down the road, we had all kinds of plans and dreams. Marc was envisioning the acres of crops he would be able to raise and the bounty of produce he would be harvesting.

I, on the other hand, collect things, primarily antique books, clocks, dolls, and furniture. That big old empty house allowed my mind to race with the thought of all the wonderful things I would be able to haul home and for which there would be no lack of room.

Yes, we had plenty of expectations for the future, and both being animal lovers who were now surrounded with open space, we knew that future would include pets of one kind or another. We had no way of anticipating, however, the large cast of characters who would find their way to our doorstep.

Chapter 2

By mid-July 1990, things were really starting to come together. The demolition was completed, all the refuse had been hauled away, and the plumbing, wiring, and new drywall were all either finished or nearly done. We had taken a break one afternoon and were in the backyard when a beautiful silver and black dog wandered up to us. He looked like a husky-shepherd cross and was so friendly and personable, I couldn't imagine he was homeless.

We, of course, made a big fuss over him and gave him some of our lunch. However, within minutes, we saw him devour a box of rat poison we had just put out.

Once we recovered from our shock, I tore up the road to our local veterinarian, Dr. Arnie Kendall. Arnie was the closest thing we had to a celebrity in town, but he would probably be quite offended to be classified in that way. Arnie, in his denim overalls, driving his old pickup with at least one or two dogs inside, was proof that all was right with at least our little corner of the world. All the farm kids in the county had Arnie stories that primarily revolved around their early barnyard experiences with castrations. After hearing many of them, I was grateful for having been raised in town. He was a no-frills guy who cut right to the point. Known for his sometimes gruff approach, he was also known for occasionally driving his patients home, opening his truck door and just dropping them off. Especially if he knew the owner was struggling financially.

I knew if Arnie was home, I could get some help. I breathlessly told him what had happened and asked what I should do. Arnie described the dog to me perfectly and said he had seen him hanging around for a couple of weeks. He then asked me where we bought the poison. If it was from the feed mill, we would have a problem, but I assured him it came from the grocery store.

His advice was to give him all the milk he would drink. I said, "That's it?"

He said that if he was a purebred, he'd be dead before long, but he was a stray so, he'd be fine. Arnie was never a fan of anything pure bred. I stopped and got milk and got him to drink as much as possible. And once again, Arnie was right. The dog didn't even seem to get indigestion. However, that was the end of poison of any kind at our house.

The dog was so gentle and loving and very well mannered, a total charmer! We did all we could to make him feel welcome and loved, hoping he would stay with us. That evening, we packed up and returned home for the night. I was sure we had seen the last of our impressive visitor, but the next day, as we pulled in the drive, he came running.

We had experienced some theft from the farm since it was no secret there was no one around at night. Once our beautiful boy moved in, however, there were no more missing tools or anything else. Marc wanted to give him a one-syllable name that was not typically given to dogs.

After much discussion and searching through a baby name book, we settled on Zeke. He and the dog both seemed satisfied with it, so Zeke it was.

Even though we were only at the farm on a part-time basis, Zeke dutifully stood guard. For the next two months, he was our lone sentry. We never once tied him or restricted his movements. He evidently had decided he was tired of wandering and was finally home.

Marc refused to ever tie a dog. He said, "If they want to stay, they will, and if they don't, there's no point in trying to keep them." It became our experience over the years they always chose to stay.

A complete gentleman, Zeke felt his primary duty was to greet any and all visitors immediately upon their arrival. He never jumped or in any way made a nuisance of himself, so it wasn't long before he was well loved by all our regular guests. My mother adored him. She found a recipe for dog biscuits and decided to give them a try. For the next twenty years, she never came to the farm without an ample supply of her famous cookies.

Zeke and all the dogs to follow quickly learned to greet Grandma's arrival with a great amount of anticipation and excitement. Three was the magic number. That's what was doled out to each and every dog. They not only learned which days to expect her, but they knew how many three were. Two were unacceptable.

About two months after Zeke came to us, our friend, Mike Smith, discovered two abandoned dogs whose owners had just moved away and left them to live in the road ditch. He had been taking table scraps to them every night but felt they would be much better off moving to our house.

One was quite young and friendly; the other exhibited signs of abuse and was scared and vicious. With that in mind, he caught the friendly one and brought him over, thinking the other one would be more manageable once he was alone.

So Skeeter became a member of our family, and a few days later, Buddy arrived. Things hadn't gone exactly as planned. The capture of Buddy required heavy leather gloves and a rope around his neck being closed in the passenger door. Once he was secured away from the driver's side, they began the five-mile journey to our house. It was reported to be a very long five miles, with Buddy lunging and snarling every inch of the way. Once they arrived, the rope was removed, and Buddy took off. I feared he was gone forever, but because Skeeter was here, he remained hidden in the underbrush along the property lines and in the woods, watching, always watching.

Buddy was, as near as we could guess, an Arnie dog. Dr. Arnie Kendall had a dog named Shiloh that fathered quite a few puppies. There were Arnie dogs all over the area for years to come and were as popular as any AKC member. Buddy was approximately twenty to twenty-five pounds, with wiry black hair, a square little nose, and ears that stood up only to droop over at the ends. He was just as cute as he was terrified. He feared all mankind and any movements we might make. A head turned in his general direction was enough cause for him to disappear for hours.

I first began trying to win him over by just walking through the yard and talking to myself. Gradually, I inched closer to the property lines, all the while keeping a steady monologue of soft words flowing. In the beginning, he predictably darted into the woods. But eventually, he began to cautiously follow along at a safe distance, still disappearing if I stopped or turned in his direction. Then I incorporated dog biscuits into my walks, occasionally tossing one into the underbrush. Once he got the nerve to try a few, I began holding them behind me and low enough for him to reach while I looked straight ahead and talked. It took days, but he eventually got brave enough to sneak up, grab the biscuit, and run. He had regular access to food and water because of the self-feeder Marc had set up in the garage and the pond water, but he seemed to enjoy the biscuits and began to take them quicker and more gently.

Buddy's friend Skeeter was a precious little soul. He looked like a miniature basset hound wearing a tuxedo on a thirty-pound body with crooked little five-inch legs. He would make regular trips out to see Buddy, but he liked the company of humans and the new batch of kittens who had recently arrived, courtesy of the outdoor cat the previous owner left for us.

It wasn't unusual to see both him and Zeke acting like old bachelor uncles gently washing the babies and entertaining them by swishing their tails.

Skeeter never could run, jump, or cover great distances quickly the way the other dogs could. Five-inch legs were not designed for great feats of athleticism. It didn't seem to bother him to always bring up the rear, and he apparently never realized that he had certain physical limitations. He went where he wanted and did just as he pleased. It only took him a little longer, always seeming to enjoy the journey as much as the destination. He would quite often be seen stopping to smell a flower or to watch a butterfly or bee going about their day.

His favorite hunting expeditions took place during haying season immediately after the hay had been baled and removed from the fields. There was always an abundance of homeless mice and moles to chase, and inevitably, there were the ones who had become the victims of the haying equipment and left for the scavengers. With those being the ones he could actually catch, they tended to be high on his list of priorities.

Life began to settle into a harmonious pattern with all the members of the family seeming contented. The only drawback was still Buddy's continuing reluctance to accept any real contact with us. It was about that time that Buddy's life and mine were both forever changed.

That particular day, I was hanging wallpaper in the kitchen when suddenly, there were horrific screams and panicked barks coming from the vicinity of the pond. The screaming sounded childlike. I dropped everything and ran! A pack of large dogs had descended on little Buddy and were viciously attacking him. Without thinking, I charged toward them, screaming and flailing my arms, which proved sufficient to scare the pack away. Buddy, who I assumed would disappear forever after all that commotion, instead came running straight to me as hard as he could come. I scooped him up and took off for the house to check him for injuries. It wasn't until I was in the kitchen with him cradled in my lap as I checked his throat and belly for any tears that I realized the situation we were in. Was he in shock? What would he do when it wore off? However, it only took looking into his soft brown eyes and seeing the love that shone there to know I had just won the adoration of the most devoted friend a person could ever hope to have.

From that day forward, he was my constant shadow. He would ride in the car, on the tractor, the hay wagon, the golf cart, in the wheelbarrow, etc. If I was doing it, so was he.

I could take him anywhere, and he would remain steadfast at my feet regardless of who else was around or what was happening.

The three dogs and I began taking daily walks down to the dead end of the road accompanied by Calico, who, as you might surmise, was a pretty little tricolored cat Marc had brought home from work. She had just shown up there and was stealing everyone's lunches. Since she wasn't winning any friends with his fellow workers, he felt she would be safer at our house. She was very cheerful and friendly and seemed to prefer the company of the dogs to that of the other cats.

With Zeke being a gray or silver color and the two little guys with their black and black-and-white markings, Cali lent some much-needed color to our little group of walkers.

Chapter 3

December 1, 1990, was moving day! I had been packing for weeks in preparation and had already hauled several carloads of our smaller possessions, but moving day still brought the last-minute push. It was a Saturday, but as things turned out, I was required to be at work and was forced to rely on Marc and a wonderful group of friends and family to handle the final details. My mom and dad were, of course, on hand, as were Marc's mom and dad. Fortunately, it was an unusually nice day for northern Ohio, because in lieu of a moving van or trailer, Marc opted for hay wagons as the mode of transportation.

There was a caravan of open hay wagons that paraded our furniture and possessions through town and out the three miles to their new home. Before that day was over, everyone in our little town of three hundred residents knew the farmhouse was completed and ready for habitation.

One of my mom's dear friends used to tell about a family she knew growing up who had many children and even more pets. Their name was Wattley, and it was not uncommon to go there and find unkempt children running in all directions, happily chased by a couple of dogs and a goat or two. Still other goats entertained themselves by playing King of the Hill with the family car. The joyful screaming children would fly through the back door, leaving the screen to slam behind them. The equally joyful goats would continue their hot pursuit, undeterred by the closed screen door. Then goats and children would all exuberantly gallop through the house and out another ill-fated screen door. On Saturdays, the crowd would load up and make their way to town with the still unkempt and raucous children hanging out every car window. Our friend said that as a teen, she used to cringe on the occasions she would find herself in town at the same time, consequently hearing her name shouted out over and over as all the family members waved energetically in her direction. For some reason, that family was on my mind all day, moving day, while I attempted to concentrate on my job. The Wattleys were moving to their new home. Time would prove that although that was the first time I felt a strong kinship with that particular household, it would be far from the last.

Summer eventually came as it always does, and Marc was in his glory, being able to actually plant the garden beds he had only, until then, been able to dream about. After seeking out a good local grower, he purchased around seventy blueberry bushes and we went to work getting them in the ground. I helped where I could, but I was also in the business of mowing lawn on my days off and many days in between, since we now had nearly ten acres to keep cut. I also began attending auctions and visiting antique shops in my quest to fill and decorate our house. It didn't take long, unfortunately, to discover that there was a limit to how much should be placed in any one home.

One morning, as I was headed out the door, I saw a movement and heard a little grunting sound. The source of the noise was a beautiful little tri-colored puppy hiding in the corner of the porch. He was much too young to have made it to the farm on his own, yet there he was. We immediately became friends, and that's when Hobo came to be part of the family. He was rough and rowdy as puppies tend to be, but the other three boys were able to keep him in line, and he never lacked for a playmate. Hobo, or Bo, grew and grew and grew, until his metamorphose was complete, from a round little pup into a gorgeous collie.

So our compliment was growing, standing now at four dogs and six cats, counting Cali and the litter of kittens. One of the kittens in particular sought out our company regularly.

She was a sweet little gray tabby with a white nose and a white bib. Having grown up with the dogs and finding Cali much to her liking, Punkin fit right into the mix. She and Cali spent many hours bathing and sunning themselves on the deck and eagerly seeking attention from anyone who chose to sit down outside for a little rest.

A pickup truck pulled into the drive one day while I was out back in the blueberry patch. Marc wasn't home, and he was the one the visitor had come to see. I recognized the man and knew he was someone I didn't really care for. Buddy seemed to pick up on my feelings and jumped to the defense. The man posed no threat to me, but Buddy was taking no chances. He planted himself halfway between us and began to growl. That was very unusual behavior for him. He normally gave everyone the benefit of the doubt. I asked the man if I could help him. He was in the market for some ripe tomatoes and had been told to check with Marc. Once I told him ours weren't ready yet, he thanked me and turned and left without incident. I didn't need defending at all, but I do feel Buddy prevented a couple of questions from turning into an extended visit, and he was rewarded.

A lost coon hound wandered into the yard one day while Buddy, Skeeter, and I were out riding the golf cart. Skeeter never liked any canine intruders and chose that moment to dive off the cart and attack. The hound, in an attempt to protect himself, made Skeeter squeal. That was all it took. Buddy then leaped off the cart and onto the hound's head.

Beginning with his ears, it appeared he intended to devour the hapless hound one body part at a time. It took some doing, but the three were finally separated, and the poor hound decided it was past time for him to leave. Skeeter had long been included under Buddy's blanket of protection.

When we had been on the farm only three or four years, Buddy developed severe pain every time he walked or ran. He would scream out in agony that was torture to hear. I took him to every veterinarian in the area, trying to find out what was causing the pain. No one seemed to have the answer. They felt it was from an old abuse injury and was just now making itself known. We were finally sent to an orthopedic specialist in Cleveland. He said back surgery should correct the problem. Several days and $2,500 later, Buddy returned home. They said it was imperative that he remain completely down for a week. I placed him in a basket, and because the first couple of days were the most critical, I carried him, basket and all, everywhere I went, including to work. I had an extremely understanding and sympathetic boss who permitted the temporary intrusion.

As long as he was placed where he could see me, he would lay quietly and blend into the woodwork. It was heartbreaking, but he lost bladder control during the whole ordeal. I had disposable diapers placed over and under him in his basket, and they, of course, needed changed a few times during the day. There was a moment that would endear my coworker, Val, to me forever. I got caught up in a very lengthy phone call with a customer when I saw Val, who was supposed to be on break, carefully changing the diapers for Buddy. After the first couple of critical days were over, I was able to leave him in his Grandma's willing and capable hands.

In a couple of weeks, Buddy's life was basically back to normal, but the loss of control severely curtailed his ability to travel with me. He would still occasionally get a jolt of pain, but it was manageable and nothing like what he had been suffering.

Chapter 4

The years passed quickly, and after giving our finances a chance for recovery, we were then able to begin making plans for the building that has come to be known as the summerhouse. It's a little cottage-type structure that we decided should be a place for Marc to store and work on his tractor. He designed it carefully and had an overhead door put in one end for easy tractor access. However, when it was nearing completion, we got the idea it would look really cute if it had a porch on it with a roof to match the porch roof on the house. It wasn't until the construction was completed that we discovered, to our chagrin, because of the height of the exhaust pipe, the tractor would no longer fit under the newly added roof. Never one to be discouraged, Marc simply repurposed the building into a place to start seeds and house his plants until he could set them outside.

We then began planning the construction of a barn with a hip roof and, of course, an overhang.

By that time, we had come to the conclusion you can never have enough cover from the elements, whether it be for equipment storage or just to sit under during a rainstorm.

At one time, there had been a barn there, but it had been completely gone for years, so now the farm was really beginning to take shape.

Marc also erected a small greenhouse originally intended for my use in growing flowers for drying and making arrangements. The first year, it was all mine to plant as much and whatever I chose. The second year, Marc began encroaching on my space, and by the third year, I was considered merely a visitor. He was starting everything from tomatoes to pumpkin plants, and he was doing very well.

The greenhouse was filled with starter trays to then be strategically placed outside. He loved to experiment, and in addition to the conventional, in the ground method, he was trying hydroponics and hanging baskets. He liked to specialize in vegetables but was willing to try anything. The only problem he ran up against was neither he nor I were any good at marketing. Being so far off the beaten path, not many people knew where he was or what he was doing. However, he started going to Saturday markets and selling anywhere he could.

One evening in May of 1996, I was waiting for Marc to get home from work. Instead, he called. "What do you feed a baby raccoon?" he asked.

I responded that I had no idea.

"Well, you'd better be finding out because you're going to have one in about forty minutes."

After a quick call to a friend who had raised several and a trip to the grocery store, One-Eyed Jack arrived. He had been named that by Marc and my brother Carl, who had found him in the middle of a busy highway, frantically circling his dead mother's body.

They thought he only had one eye, but he was so young that only one eye had opened.

In a couple of days, when the other eye made its appearance, he was shortened to Jack.

We got off to a rocky start when he adamantly refused all my attempts to get formula down him, and I spent a long night trying to comfort him while he cried and mourned for his lost mother. But with the dawn of a new day and his experiencing an empty tummy, he was willing to see what I had to offer in the line of food and make some compromises as far as the feeding devices went. I started out with a baby bottle, but that was way too big.

A doll bottle didn't meet with any more enthusiasm. The third trip to town was the charm when I brought home an oversized eye-dropper that he could suck on easily and hang onto with his front paws. It wasn't Mom, but it got the job done.

He was still very wobbly on his feet and was content to spend the first several days just eating and sleeping. That period soon ended, and he began following me everywhere. What fun he was! He was tiny, with long spindly legs that I thought gave him a spiderlike appearance. His tail was all brown and didn't look like it would ever be ringed.

I provided him with a litter box, which he took to quickly. It was easy to tell when he was using it because he would purr very loudly the entire time. It was then that the Wattley family began again inhabiting my thoughts.

Jack and I played hide-and-seek, tag, and many raccoon games I never learned the names of but that gave us hours of fun. His favorite time every day was when I made the bed. Hiding underneath, he would make a big show of jumping out and scaring me. We would then roll around and wrestle until I remembered there were other chores I should be tending to. That was never a problem for Jack. He would just help with them too.

From the first day Jack made his appearance, I had a sick feeling in the pit of my stomach.

Zeke, as wonderful as he was, liked to hunt groundhogs, squirrels, opossum, and raccoons. Occasionally, I would take Jack for a ride over to my mom and dad's. As I carried him from the house to the car and back again, Zeke would frantically dance around me, lunging for Jack as if he were a stuffed toy to be grabbed and ripped apart.

Knowing it was inevitable that Jack would have to go outside, I desperately tried to think how I could make that work and keep him safe. Although it seemed impossible at first, I began doing the only thing I could think of. I would carefully carry him out and sit down on the top step of the deck. I would then place him on my lap and quickly cover him with my body. Then as Zeke's nose poked frantically into every tiny opening, I would repeat over and over that he was our baby and we had to protect him. I was hoping with the intermingling of my scent with Jack's, he would decide he was family. I felt that was the only chance we had to make it all work out.

As Jack grew, I would take him out and stand him on the deck railing as I stood guard with my arms up for protection. Zeke would run from side to side and stand up, trying to get as close as possible. Still repeating the words, I would also pet Zeke in an attempt to keep things positive. Our outdoor visits were kept quite short for a long time. I don't think they upset Jack, but I was a nervous wreck.

Just when I was beginning to think it would never work, Zeke appeared to be getting bored with that game and with Jack. He started lying down and watching from a distance. That's when I decided it was time for Jack to learn how to climb a tree. The only climbing he was doing in the house was onto the back of the couch to catch a nap. So Marc and I took him out to the wooded area in the center of our driveway where a large limb had blown down from the maple tree. It was lying at a slant with the highest part only being about four feet off the ground. I placed Jack on the branch, and he promptly fell off. I caught him, and after six or seven tries, he finally seemed to get the hang of it. Once he could navigate the limb and then the tree, I felt he had at least one skill he could use if he were in danger.

As Jack became more mobile, my worries about Zeke began to diminish. He was still mildly interested in him, but more as a friend than a squeak toy. The true test came one day in late June when Zeke brought a new acquaintance into the yard. I had never seen that particular dog in the area and had no idea where he belonged. It just so happened that Jack was playing outside at the time. The new dog took one look and made a dive for him. Jack made it to Marc's van and attempted to hide behind the wheels. There was no way I could get to him without him being torn away from me, and the dog was intent only on one thing. The dog was extremely persistent and tried from every angle to get to poor little Jack.

Just then, Zeke calmly walked over to the offending dog and, without making a sound, lifted his lip in what looked like a snarl. The aggressor dropped to the ground and rolled over in a submissive pose. As soon as Zeke turned away, however, he resumed the attack. This time, Zeke walked over and took the muzzle of the strange dog in his mouth and held it shut for approximately three to five seconds. Upon release of his muzzle, the new dog turned and walked away, never to be seen again. With peace once again being restored to his world, Jack came back out from his hiding place and resumed his play.

That incident elevated Zeke to hero status in my eyes and playmate status in Jack's. Zeke had a beautiful plumed tail that he carried proudly curled over his back. It was sacred ground to him and was accessible to no one. As much as he loved us, even we weren't privileged enough to touch it. Actually, there was only one creature on earth with that prerogative, and his name was Jack. Zeke would stand, head and tail hung low, appearing completely mortified, while little Jack would sit on his haunches behind him and gleefully run his "hands" through the tail as if he were playing a harp. Apparently, the words "He's our baby, and we have to protect him" translated in Zeke's mind into "He's allowed to do anything he wants."

As I was awaiting the arrival of my friend Paula one morning, I walked out to the blueberry patch to see how they were ripening. She pulled into the drive about that time, and I began walking toward her. Just then, Jack came scampering out of the bushes and up the lane behind me. What had been a big smile of greeting seemed to freeze on her face, and as I got closer, she said in a very quiet monotone, "Do you realize you have a raccoon right behind you?"

Jack was the one who answered her question by standing up against my leg and reaching to be picked up. It was then that I realized how preoccupied I had become with the farm and the animals and had been out of touch with my friends.

As the summer progressed, our "baby" grew to about thirty pounds. He was still living in the house with us, but the walls were beginning to close in. His play was becoming more aggressive and more and more threatening to the household furnishings.

It was at that time I was asked to take in a four-day old kitten. I was very concerned about Jack's reaction to the new family member and didn't care to take any chances with him. It seemed prudent to turn Jack into an outdoor raccoon. The kitten and my lamps would all be much safer.

Marc had set up not only the dog feeder but one for the cats as well, which Jack was already visiting regularly. So we knew even if he wanted to take up permanent residence in the barn, he would be well fed. Jack wasn't happy about the turn of events and became quite disgusted about the back door being closed to him. It was painful to see him beg to be let in. We still romped and played together in the yard, but he continued to insist he should be inside with us.

That was when he began dropping little "amendments" in front of the door to show his disdain. In October, we saw him for the last time. I want to believe he found a mate to settle down with and raise a family. A month or two after my last sighting of him, I found another little gift in front of the door. I took it as a sign that all was well.

Chapter 5

The new kitten we took in was the result of a call from a friend. The friend had been in the process of removing a stump from his yard when he discovered too late that a cat had a new litter of kittens living under it. Only one kitten survived the ordeal and appeared to be only a day or two old. They tried to reunite it with its mother, but she no longer recognized it as her baby. It wasn't where she had left it, and they had made it a bed out of cedar chips, which had completely destroyed his scent. They were going to keep it and raise it by hand, but it had cried all day and all night, and they couldn't get any sleep.

That was how Samson came to live at our house. He looked much more like a mouse than a cat. He was only five inches long and solid gray. His head was too big for the rest of his body, and of course, his eyes were still sealed shut. He was definitely unhappy and crying at the top of his lungs. I decided the best place to start was to try to feed him.

I had already picked up some special kitten formula and, with the aid of my trusty eyedropper, started giving him as much as he would eat. The poor little thing was starved, and once his belly was full, he calmed right down and went to sleep.

So we were back on feeding schedules and being accountable to a baby. Thank heavens for my mom, for it was Grandma to the rescue once again. I worked every day, and Sam needed to eat every couple of hours, so Mom was more than happy to "kitten sit."

I would drop him off on my way to work in the morning and pick him up at night. He grew rapidly, and before we knew it, he was running all over the house. Once he was weaned, he could stay home by himself. I felt bad knowing he had to be bored and lonely, and Mom just happened to have a litter of kittens she was trying to find homes. There was one dainty little female that looked just like Sam, only smaller. She began following me around the yard at my mom's, so it was no surprise that she wound up at our house as well.

Angel seemed the most appropriate name for her. She was always the quiet and well-mannered little lady, which was the exact opposite of Sam, and they got along perfectly. She would race through the house with him and play most of his silly little games, sometimes until they both collapsed from exhaustion. If he got too rough, however, she would escape and have some quiet time.

It was that same summer that we became acquainted with a young couple who had been evicted from their apartment. They had spent the last several weeks living in their car along with a young dog. The dog was very lively and restless and needed some space to move around. Would we be willing to take her?

A young man, a newlywed who worked with Marc, happened to be with us and was immediately drawn to the dog. He said he would really like to have her; however, she would need to stay at our house on a temporary basis until he and his wife moved into their new home. So Abbey came to stay with us.

We walked her around the property lines several times and then turned her loose. She ran and ran and ran around the backyard, down the lane, along the woods, up the gas well drive, across the field, and back into the yard. I couldn't even guess how many circuits she made, but I didn't see how anything could run so fast for so long.

Abbey's stay kept being extended from week to week, and we eventually came to the realization that the new wife was not enthusiastic about the arrival of a new dog. The day finally came when we were told that her answer was "No!" So now we had Abbey, who brought us up to five dogs. She was a beautiful Australian shepherd/border collie mix (as near as we could guess) and a completely wonderful dog. She had much more energy than any of the others, and she required constant attention. A neighbor on the next road over said he would like to have her. Marc loaded her up and delivered her to his house.

By the time Marc had run a couple of errands and returned home, Abbey was here waiting for him. He tried twice more to deliver her to a new owner with the same result each time. It was at that point we decided Abbey was already home.

With Abbey's addition to the family, I noticed an obvious change in Marc's overall attitude. Four dogs were pushing his limits, but five were nudging him over the edge.

Every day, I would hear the same complaint that he couldn't walk across the yard without tripping over dogs! There was a lot of truth in what he said, and one day, I responded with "Okay, which ones are we going to get rid of?"

His answer was a lot of grumbling under his breath as he went out the back door. I knew I was safe in asking. They were all family.

We took all the dogs and cats to be spayed or neutered as soon as possible. I loved them all but didn't need to be completely overrun with them. According to Marc, everything that crossed the threshold of our yard was here until the inevitable day came when he had to dig the hole. It would only take one or two litters of anything before we were completely overwhelmed.

Marc would sometimes accompany me to the veterinarian appointments. It didn't take us long to learn that the best thing for him to do once the examination was over was to take the patient and leave the building while I paid the bill. On the few occasions when he would forget and was standing at my side when the amount of the bill was announced, we would both cringe. He always found the amount to be painful. My pain came later when I got to hear about it for the next week. He said if he didn't know the amount, it didn't bother him. That practice has worked well for all of us.

After the first few weeks of what must have seemed to her as overwhelming freedom, Abbey began to settle into more normal patterns of behavior. It didn't take long to see that she was a one-man dog, and that one man was Marc. She became his constant companion and took it as a personal affront if he chose to ride the golf cart without her.

With Marc always on the move, the golf cart became an invaluable piece of equipment. Abbey discovered right away that she enjoyed having the wind in her face and Marc at her side as they rode down the road or across the fields. She also found it quite comfortable to lie stretched out on the seat with her head on his lap. That way, there was no danger of another passenger trying to squeeze onto the seat and relegating her to the floorboard.

Marc hired teenagers as summer farm help. "Crumb snatchers," he liked to call them, and they all seemed to enjoy the use of the golf cart. By then, Abbey had come to the conclusion that any time the golf cart moved, she should be on it. She would watch intently for anyone headed in its general direction. They all learned that if they wanted a place on the seat, they had better run to beat Abbey. The kids were all great and would take her along with them or stop and pick her up in the unlikely event that she had missed getting on when they did.

One of the most memorable things about our Abbey was her bark. Extremely shrill doesn't even begin to describe it. Fortunately, she kept it to a minimum when we were home alone. We knew if Abbey was barking, we had better go see why. It was a completely different situation if we had company. Trying to carry on a conversation with Abbey around was next to impossible. She knew she was not the center of attention at that point and felt it was up to her to correct the oversight. We and any visitors who had been here more than once knew someone, anyone, had to be giving her their undivided attention. As long as she felt she was part of the visit, she was fine.

The only thing Abbey loved almost as much as Marc was a cat. Actually, all cats. By the time she came to us, we had acquired not only Calico and Punkin, but Fred, a beautiful longhaired orange cat with a fluffy white bib and white tummy, and three large black-and-white barn cats. Once Abbey arrived, she became the primary focus of all of them.

Their main goal was to guarantee she never had a moment to herself. One or the other of them was following her, rubbing on her, or at the very least lying close enough to be able to reach out and touch her. Although there were many days I saw her struggling to keep them out of her face as they persisted in rubbing on her nose, she never once lost her temper. The most she would do was get up and move out of their way. It was quite pointless though because they always hunted her down.

Not long after the barn was completed, Marc found himself with a hammer in his hand once again. We had learned of two donkeys that needed a new home, and Marc quickly constructed a large stall to accommodate the boys, Jack and Jasper. They were both sweethearts, but Jack was the more personable of the two, and it didn't take us long to get completely attached. Their welcoming brays every time we came out of the house were music to our ears. They settled in quickly and seemed to enjoy their new surroundings and all the attention they got from us and anyone who came to the farm.

Shortly after the donkeys arrived, we discovered a side of Zeke we had never before seen.

My dad was in the hospital after having some minor surgery, and Mom, my brother Carl, and I were going to visit him. I asked Marc to go along, but he said he'd wait until Gramps got home to go see him. Marc had an aversion to anything medical. So we went, and while we were sitting at Dad's bedside, a nurse came in to tell me I had a phone call. It was the emergency room in Anderson. They said they had my husband, and he was asking for me. The hospital we were visiting was forty miles away in Wentworth. Naturally, we headed for home.

By the time we arrived, Marc was back in our kitchen with his leg in a cast and propped up on a chair. His friend, Mike, was with him and still chuckling over the events of the last couple of hours. It appeared Marc was on the tractor in the back field, pulling up brush to clear the land for planting. He chose the wrong bush and uncovered a nest of very angry ground hornets. They took offense at the destruction of their home and attacked the intruder. Marc baled off the tractor, and upon hitting the ground, he snapped his ankle. In spite of that, he had no choice but to run. They still managed to get in over twenty stings before their attack ended. There he was, broken ankle, covered with stings, and his tractor, which he had left in gear, was still traveling slowly across the field. He was then forced to chase down the escaping tractor and ride it back to the house to summon help.

After getting back to the house, he had managed to hobble inside to call his friend for a ride to the emergency room. By the time we got home, he was an incredible shade of green, all puffed up from stings, and shaking like a man headed to the gallows. My heart went out to him, but the irony proved to be too much for me, and I felt compelled to say, "You do know there are easier ways to visit the hospital."

A few weeks into Marc's recovery, a stranger pulled into the driveway. Marc and Zeke were sitting on the back step when the man got out of his van and began to approach them.

Zeke suddenly leaped off the deck and got directly between Marc and the oncoming stranger. The hair on his back stood up, and he began snarling. The man retreated. Once he received the desired response, Zeke began wagging his tail, and he looked over his shoulder at Marc as if to say, "Did you see that?" The man took that to mean everything was then all right and began once again to approach

Marc. Once again, Zeke went into the defensive mode, and the man backed up. That took place three times before the man got the idea he wasn't welcome and left.

It was so hard to understand how such an amazing dog had been homeless and left to wander. He was a mystery that would never be solved.

One morning, upon my arrival at work, I discovered a little black ball of fur huddled at the office door. It took me all of three seconds to pick the puppy up and take her inside.

"Look who I found at the door!" I said to my coworkers. "I wonder what such a little girl is doing out by herself! Did any of you see her when you came in?"

They all answered in unison, "No!" Well, it was cold out, and I couldn't see her wandering out into the road or getting hurt in some other way, so I made her a bed and went to work.

It seemed likely that someone would be looking for her. She was so little I couldn't believe she made it very far from home. I felt I should be making some calls around the neighborhood on my break or put a notice in the paper. However, Lenny Kapp, whom I literally had known since kindergarten, convinced me that if anyone were looking for her, they would stop in our office, and he would keep an eye and ear open for any information about her. He lived right there in town and knew about everyone, so I thought he would be the perfect one to track down her owners. But when it came time to go home that night, no one had claimed her, so she went home with me.

It was several years later that I learned the truth about Brandy's origin. During one of the early morning discussions that would take place while we were working, someone asked me how she was doing. That didn't seem odd because they quite often would inquire about one or another of my pets.

Then Don Dwyer started laughing and said, "Well, Lenny, it's a good thing Joelle got to work when she did and the pup didn't have time to wander off." Then they all started laughing, and the truth finally came out.

Lenny had been given the puppy by a friend. Deciding rather than keep it, he would find it a good home, and what better home than mine? He knew if I found a poor defenseless little waif at the door, she would be impossible for me to resist. So he brought her to work, and they all played with her until it got close to my starting time. He then sat her outside the door just as I pulled into the parking lot. I thought it was odd that day that she kept hanging around Lenny's feet, so I tried to convince him that she should be his dog, but he just wasn't interested. I was surprised that they kept the secret for two years. It wasn't likely I would have returned her.

Brandy looked to be part Lab, black, with long square nose and the right size, but her hair was a little longer and had some curl in it. So she matched everyone else at the farm with questionable parentage, but she was still a beautiful dog. Labs have such a reputation for being water lovers, but not Brandy. Wading around the edges of the pond was her thing, just enough to cool off on a hot summer's day. She would get plenty wet, and if you happened to be standing too close when she got out, you found out just how wet.

One cold winter day several years later, Brandy didn't come when I called her. I searched the farm and the woods and drove around the area to no avail. The next step was to call the Animal Protective League and see if she had somehow wound up there. Then I notified all the veterinarians in the area and put notices up in all their offices and a few stores. Still nothing.

Then I got a call from a friend who worked at the APL saying she thought they might have Brandy. I went right up, but the dog they showed me was a much older female Lab/pit bull mix.

"No," I said, "Not the one I'm looking for." Well…that dog had been there two weeks, and no one had shown any interest in her. She was scheduled to be put down the next day. So I went back to her cage and started talking to her. I explained the situation and asked her if she would like to go home with me.

Apparently, the word *home* struck a chord with her, and she began barking and dancing around. Everyone working at the shelter came running to see what was going on because they said she hadn't made a sound the entire time she had been there.

Once the paperwork was filled out and the fee paid, we were on our way home.

Once we arrived, I realized that she had a specific home in mind and a specific person she expected to find there. She nearly trampled me trying to get out of the car, and since I had a collar and leash on her, I had all I could do to try to keep up with her as she searched the entire property, looking for her person. She jumped to look inside every vehicle. We went through every building, including the house. It was heartbreaking to see how desperately she wanted to go home. I called the shelter and asked how she came to be there. They said all they knew was she had been picked up somewhere in Anderson, a town of three hundred thousand people. Those were the days before social media, and I had no idea how to find her person short of putting an ad in the paper or just driving her around, hoping she would recognize something. I regret not trying either of those things, but I felt if she sat at the shelter for two weeks without them trying to locate her, they either had been passing through and she got away, or they didn't really want her back.

They had been calling her Duchess at the shelter, but I knew that wasn't her name, so one day on our walk, I started just calling out random names. Queenie, Sophie, Gretchen, but when I said Heidi, she stopped, whirled around, and came on a dead run. She climbed all over me in her joy to have someone know who she was.

Heidi lived out her days happily, not joyously but happily. She had us and the company of the other dogs. She had her freedom to run and hunt in the woods, but I always felt there was a separation between us. I know what it's like to have the complete love and devotion of a dog, and she had already given her heart to someone else. She had only affection left to share with us.

It was winter here in Ohio, and we had received a lot of snow over the last few weeks. It had piled up with no thaw. Once it did begin to thaw, we found Brandy buried in a snowbank. It was always painful to lose a pet, and this was no exception. Each time, Marc had to remind me that we gave them the best life we could and that they knew they were loved.

The farm had become the obvious location for most of our family celebrations, and we hosted several reunions, anniversary parties, and a couple of corn roasts. The first corn roast was a group effort, with Sam Baker manning the pit in which the corn was roasted. Jon Hanks operated the grill, and everyone contributed a covered dish. It was well attended with about fifty of our friends and relatives joining in the fun. As the hosts, we were often distracted by various things, but I noticed after it was in full swing that someone was missing.

My little Buddy wasn't by my side, and I realized I hadn't seen him for quite a while. I began scanning the area but saw no sign of him. After an hour or two, when he still hadn't made an appearance, I became quite concerned. The summerhouse was serving as the center of the party, and as I began a more detailed search, I spotted my little Buddy. There he was, perched in an otherwise empty five-gallon bucket tucked back in the corner. Apparently, the hundred plus feet had proved too much for him, and he felt more comfortable observing the crowd from a distance.

He was still in a position to see everything that went on, just from a safer vantage point.

Our various parties and reunions must have been a source of confusion to all of our four-leggeds. Having around forty or fifty people, many of whom were strangers to the animals, suddenly descend upon the farm had to have been overwhelming to them. Add that to the fact that they weren't used to more than a couple of children at a time, and there could be eight or ten racing around the yard, laughing and squealing. We had great faith in all of them and their personalities. We took the time to introduce everyone to them as they arrived, but that may have been a small comfort.

One such occasion was a family reunion, and people were everywhere on the farm. At a certain point, a toddler was running the length of the deck and laughing. Everything was going smoothly until the toddler fell and began to cry. I was crossing the yard at the time and heard crying, but suddenly Zeke was barking. I couldn't imagine what was happening so I ran!

There they were on the deck, a crying two-year-old and Zeke pacing between him and his concerned parents and barking for us to come and sort it out. He didn't know who the baby belonged to, and no one was just arbitrarily going to grab him. He wasn't threatening anyone; he just wasn't allowing anyone to cross his line of defense. All it took was for me to tell him it was all right and that no one was going to hurt the baby. Immediately the tail started wagging, and peace was restored. He was a born protector.

Chapter 6

Our lives seemed to be in a constant state of flux. Ever since we had moved to the farm, we were either constructing a new outbuilding, growing a different crop, or adopting a new pet. Marc and one of his friends got the idea of getting some fainting goats. They look like any other goats, but if startled, their bodies freeze up, and they fall over onto their side. It's only temporary, but it's their only defense mechanism. A questionable one at best.

They purchased a small herd with several pregnant females, and they were going to be kept in Mike's barn. I got a call in mid-January. It was the coldest day yet of the winter, and naturally, several of the nannies were giving birth. The temperatures were dipping into the minus ten-degree range at night. One baby had already died, and another wasn't far behind because the first-time mom had thrown it in the corner and refused to take care of it. I was on my way immediately!

There he was, lying in a crumpled little heap in the corner of the stall, lifeless. I grabbed him up, stuffed him inside my jacket, and headed for the car. Of course, those types of things always happened, in my experience, at 6:00 p.m. on a Saturday night.

I called every veterinarian I could think of and couldn't reach any of them. Finally, Dr. Brown from the animal hospital in Anderson called back, and I explained the problem.

"Where is he now, Joelle?" he asked.

"He's wrapped in a blanket…on my lap…in the recliner," I responded.

After a short pause, during which time I could actually feel him role his eyes, he replied, "He'll be fine."

He was fine, and about the cutest little critter you could find anywhere. He wasn't quite as big as our house cats, black and white, with a little tail that could register great excitement or happiness. Standing only twelve inches tall from the floor to the tips of his ears, I named him Whisper because he was no bigger than one. With him being a little too big for my trusty eyedropper, I tried a couple of baby bottles. He hated them and refused to have anything to do with them. I had some latex gloves, and after washing them out thoroughly, I put a pinhole in the end of one finger. I filled it up with warm milk and rolled the glove up to apply pressure and force some milk out the hole. He was ecstatic! That little tale went in circles. When he was really tiny, I would hold him on my lap while he ate, but as he grew, he decided he preferred to stand and kneel on his front legs as if he were drinking from Mom.

I found a good-sized cardboard box for him to sleep in, and like our little Jack, he was content in it for a week or two, as long as he could get out and play for several hours a day. Getting out to play consisted of galloping wildly through the house, scattering cats in every direction, and in general having a grand time, kicking up his heels and tossing his head at everyone.

Housebreaking a baby goat was not something I had ever given much thought to. I longed for the ease of training Jack and the kittens. I finally concluded that it was pretty hopeless. There was a reason they lived in the barn. I tried to keep track of when he had eaten and when he might need to go, and then I followed him around with an empty can, trying to catch anything that was voided. It felt as ridiculous as it sounds, and I think I only had about a 30 percent success rate. Consequently, there was a lot of floor scrubbing and carpet shampooing that winter. As anyone might guess, my thoughts during that time repeatedly traveled to the events at the Wattley family homestead. Little did I know they had blazed the trail for what had become my life.

As Whisper was playing in the living room one day, I got the bright idea of bringing in my mini trampoline for him to bounce on. It took but just a flash for him to see the potential in that. He jumped on it, bounced several times, and landed on the chair, from the chair to the couch, from the couch to the coffee table, and from the coffee table into Marc's lap. Marc happened to be eating a plate of spaghetti at the time, and as Whisper skidded across his plate, Marc's faced registered complete shock, as I'm sure mine did as well.

What a mess! I had to not only clean up the mess in the chair but also chase down an excited little spaghetti-covered goat as he continued on his circuit around the living room furniture.

Whisper soon learned about the microwave and its connection to him. I would warm his milk in it, and all the while he would stand in rapt attention, looking up with his little tail circling rapidly. When the timer would ring, he would begin bouncing and bleating. Eventually, he decided that goat chow was preferable to a diet of milk, and I had to admit that my baby was growing up.

I still didn't have the heart to transfer him from a warm house to a cold barn, so for the next several weeks, he was housed on our enclosed but unfinished and much cooler front porch. I brought in hay for a bed and for munching, and he settled in after a short period of protesting. Once the temperatures started to climb, he was transferred to the barn and put in the stall with Jack and Jasper. I was momentarily concerned they might hurt him, but that fear was laid to rest as he proceeded to ram them in the legs when they tried to get acquainted. Apparently, he would be able to take care of himself. Actually, he ruled the roost, and the donkeys learned to keep their distance.

In what seemed just a few short months, my "baby" grew into a very large and very sturdy goat. Instead of a sweet little face, he now sported a large head with massive horns, each three feet long, and a body with hair hanging down to the ground.

Whisper was never neutered because I just couldn't do that to that sweet little baby.

That's a choice I lived to regret. Never having had experience with billy goats, I had no concept of the stench that would emanate from every part of his body and only increase with age. It got to the point that if a breeze was coming from the general direction of the barn, anyone entering our property could tell immediately that a billy was nearby.

One of Marc's favorite sources of entertainment was to encourage any children visiting to pet the goat. That was all the contact necessary to guarantee the ride home for the parents would be less than pleasant. Even after a thorough handwashing, the all-pervasive odor would be only slightly lessened.

Whisper had grown to the point of becoming a menace to the farrier when he came to trim the donkey's hooves. Every time the farrier bent over, Whisper would see his opportunity and ram him. It became my responsibility to keep Whisper distracted and entertained during the trimming process. He was not easily distracted or entertained, and hoof trimming days became some of my least favorites.

On one extremely cold winter day, as we were headed out on a shopping trip, we noticed a little black cat sitting on the other side of the ditch near the neighboring farm. The snow was very deep, but she didn't seem to be in any distress, so we mentioned it and went on. Two or three hours later, on our return trip, we noticed the same little cat sitting in exactly the same spot. We decided we had better check on her.

We stopped. I opened the car door and asked her if she needed some help. The words were no sooner out of my mouth when she began frantically yowling and crying. After wading through the thigh-deep snow, I saw she had been sitting in that one spot so long, she had melted down four or five inches into the snow. She never struggled once and quietly snuggled into my arms.

We took her home, wrapped her in a blanket, and I sat with her lying on her back in my lap. Her eyes shone with such gratitude it was impossible to miss. After being looked at by a veterinarian, it was determined that her feet showed some frostbite, but he thought they would recover. However, her tail was frozen solid. He didn't hold out much hope for it surviving. We took her home, kept her warm, and made a bed for her in Marc's office above the garage.

When Marc went out the next morning, he found her playing with her tail. However, it was no longer attached to her body. That led to another trip to the vet to have her tail docked and stitched up. Marc took to her immediately and named her Stub. For the next several years, until his retirement, he and Stub happily coexisted in his office.

She had the option to come and go but chose to spend her days in his company. She had her own office chair and developed quite an attitude about her "kingdom" and anyone choosing to enter it other than Marc and me. Everyone learned to give her a great amount of respect. If she jumped in their lap, they learned to sit still. Too much moving around on their part resulted in retaliation either with tooth or claw. The same went for getting too loud or animated or either petting her too much or too little. Since no one could ever determine how much was too much, that was generally what got them into trouble.

Stubby developed quite a reputation on the farm, not only with the humans but the dogs as well. She had no tolerance for the canine community we had fostered and didn't hesitate one moment to demonstrate that fact. All the dogs learned to defer to her in any and all circumstances. Her unexpected approach was met with eyes rolled in her direction, but otherwise, a dog frozen in place. I'm suspicious they even held their breath.

By that time, Marc was traveling worldwide with his Linde Air job, training employees on doing maintenance on plants and restarting them. He didn't do all the traveling. Sometimes they brought the trainees to him. His first one was Alex from China. Of course, Alex wasn't really his name. It was the one he had chosen to use to make it easier for us to address him.

He was in the US for two weeks, and Marc had him at his side the entire time. They became quite close, and Marc thoroughly enjoyed his company. He was a brilliant young man and learned his lessons quickly. Originally, his stay was to be about ten days, but it got extended to fourteen. Because the last few days were over the Fourth of July weekend, his room was already reserved in someone else's name, and Alex had nowhere to stay. Marc called. I made up a guest room, and he stayed with us.

Marc took great delight in exposing him to our way of life. His only mode of transportation in China was a bicycle. He had never driven anything else. So Marc got out the eighteen-horse Cub Cadet and asked Alex if he wanted to mow lawn. That was a concept completely foreign to him, and not only had he never done it, he had never seen it done. So he climbed aboard and asked Marc for some direction.

Marc, in his usually helpful manner, said, "If it's green, drive over it." Poor Alex! He took off very slowly and hesitantly tried to master the steering wheel. And gradually, as his confidence increased, so did his speed. It seems second nature to us to mow in connecting rows. However, Alex just mowed. There were circles, squares, squiggly lines, and none of them connected to anything. He was so thrilled with his job, it was all we could do to get him off the mower when it started getting dark.

The next morning, I looked out at the lawn, which appeared as if the mower had been in hot pursuit of a butterfly. It looked like no lawn I had ever seen before. Alex and Marc were gone for the day, or so I thought. So I attempted to fill in some of the blanks and make it look more like a lawn. I had no sooner started than they returned.

Alex announced to Marc, "Jo is not happy with my work!"

I felt terrible, and as soon as they were parked, I took him the mower and explained the concept of lawn mowing. He gladly climbed back on the tractor and spent the next several hours evening things out.

Once he had mastered the Cub Cadet, he hesitantly asked Marc if he could possibly drive the golf cart. Marc was more than happy to continue his education, and the next thing I knew, Alex was putting around the yard. wearing the biggest grin I had ever seen. He then asked if it would be possible to take a picture of him behind the wheel so that he could prove to his friends back home that he had actually driven it. It really tugged at my heart to see him so excited and proud of something that we took so much for granted.

Alex's visit ended all too soon. Marc took him back to the airport and found it very hard to say goodbye. He said teaching Alex was much like exposing an innocent child to the wonders of the world around him.

Once Marc retired from his job with Linde Air, he closed his office and began spending most of his time working around the farm and in the summerhouse on various projects. Stubby also altered her lifestyle and spent more time outside and established her kingdom in the summerhouse. The same attitudes and rules applied, just in a different location.

My parents…correction, my dad was an avid camper. They had tented and later "trailered" ever since they were first married in 1940. Both of my brothers and I were turned into campers at very early ages. Because of all the time they spent here during that year of renovations, they both were in love with the farm. Living only eight miles down the road, they were already frequent visitors, but we especially enjoyed having them bring their motor home over and camp by the pond. Those were some of our favorite weekends. They were spent having family cookouts and evenings talking around the campfire. My brother Carl and his wife, Marlene, only lived about ten miles away, so they would also bring their motor home and join in the fun.

Those weekends were the animals' favorites as well. Grandma was never a disappointment. By bringing a generous supply of her dog treats, special treats for the cats, and of course apples and carrots for the boys in the barn, her arrival was always reason for excitement and celebration.

It took the blueberry bushes five to seven years to really begin producing, but by that time, Marc had increased the size of the patch to well over a hundred bushes. The month from mid-July to mid-August was overwhelming to me. I was still working and trying to pick in the evenings and weekends. Once they ripened, they need to be picked clean often.

We didn't have an established market, so we couldn't afford to hire pickers; and the U-pick concept needed someone to oversee it, plus our insurance agent blanched at the mention of it because of all the dogs. I wasn't available, and Marc was tied up with his other crops.

That's when our mothers offered to take over. They would come every other morning during the week by 7:00 a.m. and pick the patch clean. Marc's mom lived alone and enjoyed the social aspect of it, and sadly, by then, my dad was in the early stages of dementia, and my mom welcomed the break in her routine. Sometimes Dad would come with her, but most of the time, he chose to stay home and watch TV and write in his diary.

Our moms were such fast pickers that they were usually through by 10:30 a.m. and going on about their days. I know their main reason was just that they wanted to help because that's how they were, but anytime we went out with them, we heard a lot of laughter and nonstop conversation.

Every year, the bushes seemed to produce more berries than the previous year, which was a good problem to have, but I was soon overwhelmed with them. Marc was out of town one year when I was once again faced with that problem. I had checked with the local grocery stores, but they weren't interested, so I loaded up several cases and began driving the back roads, looking for likely berry buyers. I was doing quite well and soon found myself at an Amish farm. There were barefooted laughing children darting through the yard, and as I pulled in the drive, the parents came out to see me. Once I showed them what I had, the lady of the house went in and returned with two of the largest bowls I had ever seen. They took every berry I had left and thanked me profusely for delivering them.

The next year brought the same challenge, so Marc chose to do just what I had done.

I told him to revisit my Amish family and told him specifically which farm it was. When he arrived at their house, the owner came out and very nicely refused his berries, saying that there was a lady that brought berries to them and they would wait to deal with her. Once Marc explained that was why he was there and that lady had sent him, they again were glad to do business and were grateful for the delivery.

Chapter 7

Later that summer, shortly after Marc's return home one evening, he entered the kitchen and asked, "Did you really think I wouldn't find him?"

"What in the world are you talking about?" I asked.

"Like you don't know. That little guy you've got stashed under the bench in the summerhouse." There was no more time for questions because by the time the screen door had slammed, I was sprinting across the backyard. I really didn't have any idea who or what he was referring to, but I was sure going to find out.

It didn't take long to find the ten or twelve-week-old puppy peeking out from under the workbench. I assured Marc I knew nothing about him and quickly began making friends. Someone told us they thought he might be from the trailer on the next road. I took him to them and asked if that's where he belonged. They replied that he was their pup, but they were planning to take him to the APL the next day because they couldn't keep him. That's when Clifford joined our family.

Clifford appeared to be a hound mix. He was long legged with short, mostly white hair, and ears that could stand up but preferred not to. He had a black spot that covered one ear, and the rest of his body was decorated with a variety of assorted spots and speckles. He was quite a sight but so cute and loving. Timing was everything, I guess, and with the threat of a cage at the shelter being in his near future, he had wisely chosen that time to move down the road to our house.

Clifford became extremely popular not only with us but all of our visitors, and especially with our veterinarians and their staff. He had a way of getting himself into trouble and having to make regular and sometimes hurried trips to their office. It got so that when I would call to make an appointment for another one of the animals, the first question I would be asked was "How's our Clifford doing?"

He had a habit of smiling at us, which gave his face a near sinister look. Anyone who wasn't familiar with him and his ways could be quickly made to feel ill at ease or downright nervous. Marc, of course, thoroughly enjoyed their discomfort and attempted to teach Clifford to smile at everyone.

He grew into a good-sized and very solid dog, weighing between sixty and seventy pounds. Abbey was thrilled with Clifford because he approached everything with a joyous, playful spirit. She finally had someone to run and play with that could actually keep up with her.

The pair became a virtual menace to the life and limb of everyone else. They would race and wrestle in complete oblivion to everything around them. They bowled the other dogs and cats over on a regular basis, and if we were crossing the yard, we soon learned to be ever vigilant. Those two could and did, on many occasions, knock us off our feet.

For example, I remember the time we had planted some new trees behind the pond, and I was watering them. After saturating each tree, I would stoop at the water's edge, refilling the containers. Concentrating on the task at hand, and stooped on the bank, I saw just a flash of white out of the corner of my eye. As I flew through the air and landed in the middle of the pond, it dawned on me that I once again had been blindsided by "man's best friend." Clifford's excitement at seeing me had overtaken us both.

When I looked back toward the bank, there he was, all wiggly and happy that I'd come out to play. Dragging myself from the water, I had a few choice words for him, but it was impossible to be mad at him for long. His only transgression was his overly enthusiastic nature.

He could also be very protective. The only time we saw him in action was the day we were in the field beyond our house, picking squash. Our friend, Bob Haines, after parking his truck in our driveway, suddenly appeared walking toward us. He evidently startled Clifford, and he squared off with the intruder and began barking and growling. Bob was undeterred and only had to say, "Clifford, what's the matter with you?" to start the tail wagging and the head being hung in embarrassment. I feel it would have been a much different outcome had it actually been a stranger.

Marc's horticultural endeavors continued, with his methods constantly changing and developing. He had managed to buy and erect a very large hoop house that was forty by sixty feet and was keeping it full from early spring until fall. It was a real treat for the eyes during the months of March and April because of the rows of the nearly a hundred hanging baskets spilling over with petunias, Bacopa, ivy, etc. He had found a market for them as long as they were ready by Mother's Day each year, and he worked very hard guaranteeing that they were.

He had quit using the hydroponics method in favor of raised beds and tire gardens. He also began experimenting with gutter gardens for the smaller items such as lettuce and other salad greens. One of his favorite projects were pond gardens. He would take a tire, attach a plywood base to it, fill it with soil, and plant it full of petunias. He would attach a rope and anchor it in place. It was beautiful to look out across the pond and see six or seven vibrant spots of color floating peacefully on the water. The hours he spent every morning pouring over the internet and researching seemed to be paying off.

His favorite crop to raise became garlic. Once it was in the ground, it was virtually maintenance free and always in demand.

A breakfast outing one morning led to the discovery of a tiny kitten roaming the restaurant parking lot and crying. Naturally, I picked her up and took her inside to ask if anyone knew where she belonged. The waitress said she lived next door, but she had been in the parking lot for a day or two, and she was going to get hit. I took her to the house and knocked on the door for several minutes. There was no car in the drive and no response to my knocks. I left with the kitten in tow. I took her, expecting it to be temporary and that I would return her in an hour or two.

The kitten and I made several trips to the house for a couple of days with no sign of an owner. There was no food or water left outside for her, and she had no shelter. She appeared to be only about eight weeks old, and there was no way I was going to put her down and walk away. She was a beautiful gray longhair with white rims around her eyes and faint darker gray stripes. Sassy, as she came to be known, was a real little beauty. She carried an air of superiority, clearly feeling her breeding far surpassed anyone else's on the farm.

By that time, we had lost our little Angel to cancer, and Sassy became Samson's housemate. They weren't kindred spirits like he and Angel had been, but they got along and coexisted.

Because we lived in a very old house with a natural stone foundation, and we sat very near a creek, we knew we had a snake or two in the basement. I had never seen one, but I had seen a skin every spring. Our washer and dryer were in the basement as well as the cat's litterboxes, so the door to the basement was left open.

Sassy turned out to be an avid hunter, and the basement seemed to be her favorite hunting ground. I was good with that because she took care of any mouse problem we might have had.

Unbeknownst to us, mice were the least of our basement inhabitants. One morning, when Marc went to the kitchen to make his coffee, he yelled for me to come quick. There, on the kitchen linoleum, laid what looked like a dead snake. It had been worked over pretty thoroughly, and if it wasn't dead, it soon would be. Snakes were Marc's least favorite thing, so the job of removing it fell to me. That was no problem. As long as they're not poisonous, they don't really bother me.

By the end of March that year, I had removed twenty-three snakes from the kitchen floor. Sassy was working overtime. As near as we could figure, she brought them to the kitchen because they skidded across the linoleum much better than the basement concrete, and she could still play with them long after they were dead.

By the time I got to them the next morning, most looked as though they had been through an ordeal, but seldom were they dead. Since it was March and still quite cold in Ohio, I couldn't just put them outside; however, Marc's greenhouse was heated and seemed like the perfect solution. All went well until the day he realized what I was doing. But by that time the weather had warmed enough that I didn't feel too bad about leaving them at the base of a tree or next to an outbuilding.

I was thrilled to be ridding the basement of them, but at the same time I was horrified of the fact that they had been there in the first place. Sassy's hunting expeditions were much less fruitful after that, a fact that greatly relieved me. We still had the basement walls skim coated with concrete to help deter any other visitors.

Chapter 8

"**T**HE DONKEYS ARE OUT!"

How many times, I wonder, have I heard that alarm echoing up the staircase at 6:00 a.m.?

I can remember, as a little girl, hearing the words "The cows are out!" and being filled with glee. My brother Carl lived just down the road from us and raised polled Herefords for a short time. As a ten-year-old, I enjoyed nothing more than spending a Saturday morning chasing cows. It always proved to be eventful and, in my young mind, fun. Those feelings did not carry over, however, into capturing escaped donkeys.

In the early days, as beginners, we thought the only way to catch errant donkeys was to chase them down and herd them back to their pasture. That practice only resulted in us running after trotting donkeys who stayed *just* maddeningly out of reach. On the fourth or fifth trip around the property, they would line up with the open gate and appear to be giving up, only to veer suddenly at the very last second. After several hours of what they obviously felt was highly entertaining fun, they would finally just trot back into the pasture. The phrase "less is more" must have been coined by a donkey owner. After several strenuous workouts, we eventually began to get the idea. The last time I discovered them out on my way to do morning chores, I simply walked past Jack, asked him what he was doing on that side of the fence, and continued on to the barn. After making sure their gate was open, I proceeded to pour their grain in the feedbox. They must have decided the "jig was up," their fun was over, and they didn't want to miss breakfast, so they wandered back into the stall.

The donkeys had another stablemate, a beautiful sorrel mare name Sabrina. Sabrina came to us after being forced to exist in solitary confinement for three months in a very old, very small milk house. After seeing her prison, I had serious doubts it allotted her enough room to lie down or to even turn around. Her owners had boarded up the windows, so she was in total darkness day and night and was left to only imagine the horrors that surrounded her and caused whatever noises, both soft and loud, that invaded her cell. She was removed from her confinement two or three times during that ninety-day period and "bathed." Her baths consisted of being soaked down with a garden hose before then being returned to the darkness.

The next-door neighbor could tolerate it no longer and paid her owners to release her into his custody. He then borrowed a horse trailer and delivered her to us. She understandably was in a very emotionally damaged state, and like Buddy, she trusted no one.

For the first several months, she would retreat to the farthest wall of her stall and press herself against it whenever a human entered the barn. Marc built her a very large stall, feeling she not only needed but deserved as much space and freedom as we could give her.

He also cut a door in the side of her stall that stayed open most of the time so she could go outside at will.

My horse experience was limited to trail rides on rented horses, the horse a friend loaned us one summer just for fun, and the Shetland pony I had as a little girl. Marc had even less. Sabrina needed professional handling and training, but we were nearly all she got. I watched John Lyons training videos, bought books, and avidly watched any horse training shows I could find on TV, but I realized I was completely out of my depth.

I reached deep into my experiences with fearful and distrusting animals and went back to the tried-and-true method of moving slowly, whispering, and keeping a steady flow of words. Sabrina eventually learned it was safe to advance close enough to stretch and reach my extended hand and retrieve the treats I offered. Weeks later, she would approach and stand close by as long as I made no attempt to touch her. In time, she permitted petting and brushing but was severely head shy. I found it impossible to replace the halter she had by then ripped from her head and was unable to control her in any way.

We did locate a young lady in the area, Barbara Harris, who was studying to be a trainer. Barbara agreed to take on the challenge, and Sabrina spent most of one summer with her.

I felt the greatest accomplishment of that summer was when Barbara managed to correct most of the head shying. In spite of the harsh treatment she had experienced, our Sabrina was a gentle soul. She never bit or even threatened to kick. She tolerated my trial and error methods of gentling and calming and always forgave my lapses in judgment. I had been as careful as possible to avoid scaring or upsetting her. Her state of mind seemed fragile in so many ways that I was never sure how she would react if I did badly frighten or thoroughly frustrate her.

One day, while I was in the stall with her, she seemed fine. I had been petting and brushing her when she suddenly whirled around and raced to the farthest wall of the stall. Instantly, she was rearing, bucking, kicking, and in general throwing a major tantrum. It ended as suddenly as it had begun, and she calmly walked back up to me for more petting. Seconds later, she again whirled around, and once she was as far from me as she could get, she resumed the rearing, kicking, and jumping. After about fifteen or twenty seconds of craziness, she came right back to me. That happened three times, each time just like the last. I never did figure out the cause of her actions, but they told me that even if she was scared or frustrated, she would always take my safety into consideration. Once again, I saw the gratitude of a rescued animal to those who loved and cared for them. Our bond grew, and before long upon, seeing me entering her pasture, she would run to greet me and follow me wherever I went. Hearing her soft knickers of welcome as I approached the barn always warmed my heart. She reached the point where I could lie across her back, but I never did get to ride her, which had been my goal.

Years earlier, I had been diagnosed with trigeminal neuralgia, which is severe facial pain, and I had a Teflon pad implanted at the base of my brain in an attempt to relieve the pain. The surgeon told me at the time to avoid any sharp jarring or snapping of my head and neck. As much as I wanted to ride her, I thought better of it. That and the fact that Marc never passed on an opportunity to remind me I was no kid anymore.

Sabrina's hoofs were in need of trimming, and Jon and Alana Hanks offered to take her along the next time their horses went to the farrier. When the day came, we led Sabrina out of the barn, across the yard, and nearly up to the horse trailer. Once she realized we planned to get her in the trailer, she balked, shied, reared, and went a little crazy in general. After many failed attempts, Jon asked Alana to go get Buck. Alana took off with the trailer, and as it disappeared out of sight, Sabrina calmed down and began grazing, thinking she had made her point.

About twenty minutes later, we heard the trailer once again thumping down the road. Sabrina's head shot up, and she began dancing and jerking on the lead, trying to rip it out of Jon's grip. As Alana pulled in the drive, Sabrina was extremely agitated when suddenly, Buck, Jon's horse, whinnied.

Sabrina froze! Her head and ears shot up, and they began whinnying back and forth. The trailer door was barely opened when Sabrina lunged toward it, nearly jerking poor Jon off his feet. She ran to the trailer with Jon having to really stretch his long legs to keep up. What a few minutes earlier had seemed an impossible feat now was no challenge at all as Sabrina took one leap and landed inside with Buck. Once they had her secured in a stall, she peered out the window at me as if to say, "You should have told me there would be men!" She was on her best behavior the rest of the journey.

As I was returning home from a friend's house one summer evening, I saw a dog standing on the railroad tracks a mile from our farm. Something about the way he looked at my car told me he was in distress. When I stopped and opened the car door, he bolted away.

Not going far, he turned to look at me, but when I asked if he needed help, he ran again. A car was coming, so I was forced to continue down the road. The tracks ran along our friends Jon and Alana's property. As I neared their drive, I noticed several familiar cars and trucks parked there, one of which was Marc's. A group of our friends had spontaneously gathered at the end of the driveway and were talking and laughing. As I pulled in, I heard one of them say to Marc, "I told you that was your wife!"

Marc seemed less than thrilled to see me, and I realized it was because he knew what was coming and wasn't looking forward to increasing the canine branch of the family.

Undeterred, I parked the car and walked back toward the young chow. Again, he avoided me but refused to leave the tracks. Dogs will stay where they're dropped just in case their people come back for them. I sat down in the road and began my routine of talking softly and looking off into space. He crept up behind me until I could feel his nose touch my back. As I continued to talk and coax, it became clear he wanted to trust me, but his fear outweighed it.

After several minutes of circling me, he finally walked over and looked closely into my eyes. Then, to my surprise, he collapsed into my arms.

Never before had I experienced such a sudden turnaround in a frightened animal. I'm quite sure it was due to his age. He appeared to be a puppy, possibly only four to six months old, and he was bereft of anything or anyone that was familiar. After hugging and loving him up for a few minutes, I stood and asked if he wanted to go with me.

He then followed as if he were leashed and trained to heel.

When we reached the drive, our friends proceeded to tell me the little bit of his story they knew. He and another dog had been dropped on the tracks the previous morning. They said they were willing to keep the hound that had been dropped, but not the chow. Earlier in the day, the pup had found his way to their other dog's food dish. When Jon came out of the house and surprised him, the pup had snarled at him. They didn't want him around. I had heard that chows had a tendency to be aggressive and wasn't sure I wanted to take one on either. As they loaded him in my car, however, all my protests seemed to fall on deaf ears.

Marc and I took him home, introduced him around, and walked the property line a few times. We then showed him where the feeder was in the barn. He dived in, and when one of the other dogs approached him, he viciously attacked her. A serious red flag went up, and my usually quiet little inner voice began screaming in my ear.

For the next week, every time food entered the picture, if any of the other dogs got too close, they got jumped, and a fight ensued. I asked veterinarians and a friend who worked at the APL if they thought he could be taught that was unacceptable behavior. Most of them said just because he was food aggressive didn't mean he would be generally vicious. That didn't make me feel much better, but he had been so sweet that night on the tracks, he deserved a chance.

Once he had the first week or two of being able to eat whenever he wanted and learned he no longer had to fight for food, his aggression seemed to melt away. That came as a huge relief to everyone, especially poor little Abbey, who liked to slip in and pick up any morsels the other guys dropped as they ate.

Then we had the seemingly unending challenge of a name for our friend. I wanted something regal and equal to his proud bearing. As usual, Marc had other ideas.

Our new friend had the uncanny ability to attract dirt. After only a few days on the farm, he was matted, smelly, and quite often carried sticks and leaves around in his fur. Marc was coming up with countless names, all seeming better suited to a pig. One night, he came home and triumphantly announced that we should name him Pumba.

Hmmmm. I knew I'd heard that name before but couldn't think just where. I did kind of like the sound of it, so Pumba it was. It wasn't until a couple of days later that it came to me where I had heard it. The warthog in the *Lion King*!

Oh well.

Pumba grew to be a very beloved member of the family. Mild mannered and gentle, he would stand back and wait to be coaxed up. One of the things that bothered both Marc and me was that for the next year or two, every time Marc or any man reached for him, he would cringe and seem to expect a blow. He preferred the company of women, which was obvious from the very first night. As if dumping him on a railroad track wasn't cruel enough, he had been exposed to some very harsh treatment.

We considered taking him to be sheared because once the temperatures reached sixty-five to seventy degrees, he was roasting. I asked one groomer if she was willing to clip him, and she said normally she wouldn't work with chows but would make an exception for us. I knew it wasn't something she wanted to do, so I tried it myself. He would have nothing to do with the clippers, so I got out an old pair of shears and started hacking away. He would stand or sit very patiently for twenty minutes or more. When he'd had enough, he would just move away.

After a break of several minutes, I would try it again, and he would give me another fifteen or twenty minutes. Eventually, we would succeed at cooling him off, but he then looked like one of the Berenstain Bears.

Our donkey Jasper began exhibiting strange behavior in his advancing years. He would walk in circles for hours at a time, sometimes even bumping into the walls of his stall as if he couldn't see them. Or I would hear banging noises coming from the barn, only to discover Jasper battering his head against the wall or gate. It was all I could do and sometimes more than I could do to get him to stop. I did find that rubbing his ears and talking softly to him would sometimes calm him enough to end the battering. After several minutes of that, he would gradually begin returning to his normally mild-mannered self.

We were told he was having seizures and that there was nothing to be done for him.

I scoured the internet for information and talked to some parents of children who had seizures. Once I got the name of one of the medications prescribed to humans, I asked the vet about giving it to Jasper. They were unwilling to prescribe it since it isn't normally used on large animals. I kept searching for an answer, but none was ever forthcoming.

One day, upon entering the barn, I discovered Jasper with his two front feet in the watering trough. He was struggling to escape but was getting nowhere, and I feared he would be injured in the process. Since Marc happened to be out of town, I didn't know what to do.

There was no way I could get him out alone when suddenly, I heard a truck engine and saw Jack Carn and one of his hired hands driving in the field across the road. When they looked up and saw me running across the furrowed field toward them, they had to know there was a problem. They agreed to come and help, and within just a few minutes, they had Jasper free.

There were many such incidents with Jasper over the next couple of years. He broke down the fence one night and wound up at the farm that was half a mile down the road. They had him tied to a gate when Marc found him the next morning. It took us most of the day to get him back home and in his stall. Neither he nor Jack had ever led well under the best of circumstances, and when Jasper was having seizures, he was even more difficult to control. They finally loaned us the use of their horse trailer and hauled him home for us. The poor guy was miserable a good share of the time, and it was no real surprise when I discovered he had passed away one night.

The morning I found Jasper, Marc was again out of town. I was heartbroken and had no idea how I was going to handle the situation. I called our friend Bob Haines, who lived just down the road, and asked him who I should call or what I should do.

He said, "Just go back in the house. I'll take care of it." When I objected, reminding him he had planting to get done, he said, "Some things can wait. Others can't." So he and Jessie Johnson and Brad Winters took care of everything. Good friends are a true blessing.

Jack was so lonely without him, especially since we had lost Whisper a few months earlier.

Sabrina was in the next stall, but she and Jack had never bonded. True to the natural order of things on the farm, however, Jack wasn't alone for long. A friend who worked with the Human Society had just rescued a pair of donkeys who then needed a home.

They were already named when we got them, so Pickles and Gerkin joined the clan. They were standard donkeys, a gray/brown color with a dorsal stripe, or cross on their shoulders. The move didn't seem to affect them too much, and they settled in with no problem. They had each other, and it didn't take Pickles long to fall madly in love with Sabrina. Once she entered his life, his brother, Gerkin, was simply a sidenote. Pickles stood as close as he could get to Sabrina in the stall even though there was a separation between them. Sabrina never even seemed to notice poor little Pickles and went about her day as if nothing had changed. That was in complete contrast to the little donkey's world, which now began and ended with a beautiful sorrel mare. The only time he would leave her side was when she went out to pasture and he was given no choice. She had her own section, and the donkeys all shared another section of pasture. Once she returned to the barn though, Pickles would resume his post next to her stall.

The new donkeys seemed quite young, and it appeared their brays weren't fully developed. That became more and more clear at chore times, when they would squeak and squawk in their anticipation of being fed. They sounded much like pubescent young boys whose voices had turned on them. But as the months passed, they began to gain more control. Jack set a good example for them since we had been told on a clear night that he could be heard over a mile away. In time, the little guys worked and worked until one day, I mistook Pickles's bray for Jack's. Gerkin was still struggling, but he appeared to me slightly younger than Pickles, so his day would come.

Abbey had been with us so many years. She was as constant and dependable as the sunrise and set. Her love for the cats never faltered, but in her later years, there was one cat in particular who seldom left her side. For some reason, he had never been given a name of his own and simply came to be known as Abbey's Cat. We could see the unmistakable signs of age settling on her as they do on all of us. The last couple of summers, we took her on as many long golf cart rides as we could, fearing that they would soon be coming to an end. So the morning Marc came in and told me that Abbey was gone came as no shock, just an overwhelming sadness. When I looked outside, I could see her curled up in her bed, with her companion still at her side. It was only a few weeks later that Abbey's Cat went to join her. The loyal and steadfast friends in life would remain companions forever.

Abbey has been gone quite a few years now. That little girl with, all her craziness and shrillness, who we tried and tried to give away, had instead found her way into our hearts and is still greatly missed by the couple who grew to depend on her and to love her.

Chapter 9

Heading out to the hayfield in August of 2009, Marc and his helper thought they heard kittens crying. They conducted a perfunctory search, came up with nothing, and went on their way.

As they stopped with the baler at Bob Haines's house for some quick repair work, it didn't take Bob's four-year-old granddaughter any time at all to locate the sound. Climbing onto the baler, she opened up the bale chamber and peered inside to find three two-week-old kittens.

As she began filling her arms with the little balls of fluff, Marc decided he had better get them back to their mother.

He brought them back to the machine shed, placed them in a box, and placed the box right where the baler had been parked. We checked several times during the afternoon and evening, finding the box to be gradually emptying out. On our last check for the night, we found there was still one baby left on the bed of hay. Thinking she would be back to claim him as well, we turned in for the night. Early the next morning, I rushed out to the shed to make sure she had them all, only to be met with the anguished cries of the one lone kitten.

Such a pathetic little creature with his frantic squirming and blind search for the familiar little bodies that were his only world to that point, and his empty little tummy gnawing relentlessly at him. His cries for help had gone unanswered for so long. He was beginning to give up hope. They wouldn't go unanswered for much longer. I knew where there was an eyedropper with his name on it. I cuddled him all the way to the house, trying to soothe some of his fears but possibly only intensifying them. Once the eyedropper came into play, with the kitten formula that I now always had on hand, and his belly was full, he calmed and decided things in general were looking up.

He was a tiny brown tabby with a beautiful tan-colored tummy. I named him Tigger and found out in a few short weeks how appropriate the name was for him. As he grew, instead of walking or running, he basically bounced everywhere he went.

Once Tigger got used to his new surroundings, he began to thrive. The biggest challenge was getting him filled up. The next biggest was keeping him that way. Snuggling was his next favorite thing. As he curled tightly up under my chin, I would whisper in his ear. It came as no surprise that he became rather spoiled and grew into quite a little tyrant, expecting his every wish to be fulfilled without delay.

When Tigger was five weeks old, I got the opportunity to go on a two-week Alaskan cruise with a group of my friends. That was more than I could pass up, and once again, Grandma was willing to babysit. While I was gone, she weaned him and had played with him so much that he had been transformed from a sweet, cuddly, dependent little ball to an independent, rowdy little buzz saw. He had the impression that every time my hand moved, he should attack it. It took a while, but I finally got him calmed down again and could handle him without having to keep a Band-Aid in my pocket. Grandma had become a questionable influence.

I couldn't understand why the mother cat had taken the other two babies and left Tigger to fend for himself. It was years later, after many violent fits of coughing, that I began to think she knew there was something wrong with him and had winnowed him out. I finally videoed one of the coughing attacks and showed the veterinarian. He was diagnosed with asthma and prescribed steroids.

Our canine branch of the family had aged and dwindled down to the point where Pumba was the only one remaining. We heard about an eighteen-month-old Lab mix that desperately needed to be rehomed. She was living in an apartment with three small children, and things weren't going well. We never received any more information than that, but when Sadie arrived, I could see there had been problems. She was very fearful, shaking, and when I tried to scratch her ears, she screamed! Later, I found out that the cartilage in her ears had been broken down, and she had nerve damage. So any touching of the ears became taboo.

She looked like she was equal parts Lab and shepherd with something else thrown in.

When she first arrived, I took her for the customary walk around the property lines and began to get acquainted. She and Pumba hit it off from the beginning and were always seen in each other's company. Sadie, like Pumba preferred women to men, and it soon became apparent that I was her human of choice.

It was August of 2010 when my beloved father passed away, and six months later, my mother joined him. The last few years had been extremely difficult for all of us.

Alzheimer's is appropriately termed the "long goodbye" and forces everyone connected through a maze of emotions. My dad reached the point of no longer knowing who I was, but he did know I was someone he loved. My every visit was met with him coming to the door with a huge smile, and his arms flung open wide for a big hug. I miss that so much. My mom was, unbeknownst to us, suffering from cancer but refused to get treatment because she had to stay close to my dad. They had been such a huge part of our lives that they left quite a void. The only comfort was that they were still together and no longer suffering.

My parents had a cat named Timmy whom I had never really spent any time with, and we had never bonded. I, of course, would see him and pet him when I visited, but he hung pretty close to my mom.

When our mom was in the last stages, my brother Bret and his wife, Fran, came from Virginia to be with us. After Mom passed, they stayed to help with the arrangements and for the funeral. They stayed at Mom and Dad's and cared for Timmy. When it came time for them to head home, Timmy needed a place to go, so I scooped him up.

My greatest regret with him was that we had not become better acquainted years earlier.

After a few days at our house, he came out of his shell and began showing us that he was brimming over with personality. He joined in everything that went on in the house, got along well with Tigger, and became our "greeter." Anytime we received a visitor, Timmy was the first one at the door and accompanied them to a seat. He seemed to feel it was his duty to welcome everyone and to keep them company for a few minutes after they first arrived. He was never pushy, just a sweet little presence.

I thoroughly enjoyed having him around, not only for his personality but because he was a link that remained to my parents. Sadly, just a few short months later, he passed away too.

My heart was broken from losing the joy he brought to our home and from the feeling that my parents were truly gone at that point.

Life returned to a semblance of normalcy until the day Marc suffered a stroke. He had experienced a mild one several years earlier that fortunately left him with no lasting effects.

He wasn't as lucky the second time, and his left side was the victim of some long-term paralysis. He could still walk, but slowly and with a cane. The days of him being constantly on the go from dawn to dusk were over.

We continued to run the farm and care for the animals, but on a much smaller scale.

His acres and acres of plants were reduced to a small greenhouse and several raised beds.

He could still drive the tractor for haying season, but we began relying heavily on the help of friends to get the hay into the barn. We finally decided after a few years of them generously donating their time and labor that we had to find homes for Sabrina and the three donkeys.

One of the veterinary assistants that I had become acquainted with wanted the donkeys, and a few weeks later, I found a young woman who wanted to take Sabrina.

It went completely against the grain of our lives, to send any of our loved ones away, but life changes and circumstances change, so we have to be able to adjust and change with it.

Just when I was thinking our rescue days were behind us, my niece called one evening and said she had a kitten who had evidently been hit in the road and whose left front leg was dangling.

Could I take it? We made arrangements for her to drop him off the next morning, and by the time he arrived, we had just enough time to make it to his noon appointment at the vets.

They took x-rays and examined him, but the leg was so damaged it didn't look like it could possibly heal. We decided the best solution was to remove it.

Trey, as he came to be known, looked to be about two months old, pure black, and a pathetic sight with his coned head and his half-shaved body with a rivulet of stitches. I felt so bad for him and hoped he would heal and be able to overcome his disability quickly. I had no idea of the personality I was dealing with, and I was not prepared for how quickly he would bounce back.

Sure, he was a little sluggish for a few days, but within a week, he was hopping all over the place.

We kept him secluded from Sadie and Tigger on our now completely finished front porch to give him a chance to heal in peace. The door between the house and the porch was glass, and Sadie and Tigger spent quite a bit of time peering through the door at their new brother. It can be challenging introducing a new male cat into a home already dominated by a male cat. If they get off on the wrong foot, there can be spraying incidences. Tigger had been the sole cat in the house for ten years. He was set in his ways and used to his sedentary lifestyle. I was uneasy about rocking the boat.

I took a couple of weeks to slowly introduce everyone and get them used to each other before I turned Trey loose. Once his cone was off and the stitches removed, I gave him a few more days of recuperation and then opened the door and let him go. He was a little leery of Sadie at first, but she was so gentle that he relaxed and began to show his true colors.

Trey was the highlight of my gloomy winter days, especially during the pandemic, but he was also an instigator. Suddenly, my once lazy, aging Tigger was seen regularly racing through the house right behind the troublemaker, and they would fall together in a wrestling hold. Trey had given his older brother a new lease on life. One minute they were growling and sparring, and the next they were curled up together on the bed.

Trey still obviously enjoys his relationship with Tigger, but his favorite pastime is annoying poor Sadie. She has learned that cats can be unpredictable and dangerous after spending years skirting around Stubby. Trey spotted that chink in her armor right away and uses it to his complete advantage.

Sadie just gets settled down comfortably on her bed, and Trey starts hopping toward her. She immediately begins to growl and bark at him, but we all know it's hopeless. He lays down on the floor and wiggles and rolls until his head is resting on her bed. He continues to inch closer and closer until he can touch her. He pats her gently a few times, and then he literally digs in. She yips and vacates her bed, which he then stretches out on and revels in his conquest.

He knows exactly how to wield that one front foot full of toenails, and Sadie doesn't argue with him. We now have two dog beds at opposite sides of the room so that she has a secondary retreat.

Even Trey can't guard them both.

Trey was born a thrill-seeker with a touch of Evel Knievel thrown in. He views an empty laundry basket as a portal to adventure. Any time I near one, he leaps in and hunkers down as he peers through the slats expecting to be carried from one end of the house to the other. An office chair on casters is his very favorite thrill ride. The faster it's pushed and the more it's spun, the happier he is. The sound of the sweeper brings him on a dead run so that he can play chicken with it, daring it to touch him. The truly dangerous part of that game is that he's nearly trampled in Marc's and every else's rush to get as far away from it as they can. Trey's days are spent following and sometimes chasing me through the house. He seems to feel that I require his assistance in all of my daily chores.

This last summer, Stubby looked like she was losing ground. She lost her appetite and was getting listless. I took to her to the vet, and they had a miracle salve that once it was applied to the cat's ear, they would eat everything they were given. I was thrilled that Stubby was eating and begging for more. The next day, I had applied the salve and given her supper. She seemed good and ate it right down. I was cooking our dinner and stopped to go out and check on her. It had only been about twenty minutes since I had fed her, but when I called her, she didn't move. When I went over to see what was wrong, I saw she was gone. It wasn't totally unexpected, given her age of sixteen or seventeen years, but once she started eating, we hoped she was on the mend, however temporarily. It never gets any easier.

With the loss of Stubby, looming before Marc, was the prospect of a long lonely winter in the summerhouse. That has become his daily retreat and his workshop for whatever his current project may be. We were asked to home a couple of brother and sister kittens last fall and felt they would be good companions for him, so Tinker and Tommy joined the family.

They're both little black and whites with very similar markings. We often have to look twice to tell them apart.

Though they were both wild and skittish at first, they have grown to be extremely loving and are especially attached to Marc. He has provided them with two cat beds and a separate three-tiered cat tower with scratching posts, with an enclosed level and with an open lounging area. They also have their own cat door, full-time food and water, a litterbox, and central heating. They seem to be content. They aren't the only ones that are attached.

Sadie has become my constant companion and takes it very personally if I quickly run outside and neglect to wait for her to accompany me. She lays where she can see me at all times. However, if I'm working in the house and constantly on the move, she lies in front of the back door to guarantee I don't get outside without her. She insists that I accompany her on at least two walks a day, even though she's free to come and go at will. Evidently, it isn't the same unless I'm there. We now have a third walking companion in the form of little Tinker. She insists on walking with us on the way out but likes to be carried home.

The main reason I sat down to tell this story was to fulfill one of the last things asked of me by my mom. She felt the animals' stories needed to be told. Our lives, like everyone's lives, have taken many twists and turns we could not have predicted. Some were heartbreaking, but many were wondrous gifts that caught us by surprise. I began this with the quote from Hebrews 13:2. We feel we have entertained many angels over the years. December 1, 2020, marked our thirtieth year on the farm.

We were greatly blessed with the opportunity to share our home with so many little souls who gave their love and companionship freely and completely. They have enriched our lives beyond measure.

One of the constant features we saw was that once rescued, an animal never forgets. Their appreciation cannot only be see with the eyes but felt with the heart. My hope is that as a result of reading our story, someone will reach out to an animal in need, whether it be a stray or in their local shelter. If one more animal is given a second chance at a healthy, happy life, I will consider my efforts to be successful.

I hadn't thought of it for many years until I started writing this, but as a little girl, I remember seeing the Disney movie *Thomasina* for the first time. My favorite character was the witch woman Laurie who lived in the woods and befriended all the wild creatures. She had an uncanny ability to gentle and soothe them as she nursed their illnesses and healed their wounds. I thought at the time there could be no more perfect life. I make no claim to have her magical abilities, but it would appear that not only did Marc's dreams come true on the farm, but mine did as well.

I would like to end this with a popular version of the original starfish story found in *The Star Thrower*, a collection of essays by the writer and naturalist Loren Eiseley in 1978:

> One day a man was walking along the beach when he noticed a boy picking something up and gently throwing it back into the ocean. Approaching the boy, he asked, "What are you doing?"
>
> The youth replied, "Throwing starfish back into the ocean. The surf is up and the tide is going out. If I don't throw them back, they'll die."
>
> "Son," the man said, "don't you realize there are miles and miles of beach and hundreds of starfish? You can't make a difference."
>
> After listening politely, the boy bent down, picked up another starfish, and threw it back into the surf. Then, smiling at the man, he said…"I made a difference for that one."

Grandma's Dog Cookies

Mix 2 C flour
      1 C water
Add 1 C flour
      1/2 C oil
      1/2 C honey
      1/2 C peanut butter

Add 2 tsp baking powder to next 2 ingredients and mix in with the dough

      1/2 C wheat germ
      1/2 C rolled oats
Add flour as needed and add meat scraps
Drop spoonsful onto cookie sheet
Bake 350 degrees 20 mins.
Let stand in oven 1 he with no heat and the door open.
Makes 33-38 cookies

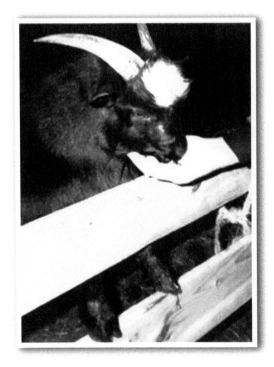

About the Author

The author and her husband share their small Ohio farm with their family of four-leggeds and, in one case, a three-legged. They are now both retired, and they enjoy a quieter and more relaxed lifestyle.

CPSIA information can be obtained
at www.ICGtesting.com
Printed in the USA
BVHW021310151121
621697BV00015B/553

9 781662 449536